from Lauren

Lauren's Life Lessons

D0869480

By Patrice M. Domozych

For Lauren's First and Goal Foundation

www.lfgf.org

DEDICATION

For Lauren and her family –

John, Marianne, and Grace

You've inspired us to live a full life; to love, think and cry… and to have a lot of laughs!

I love you

XO Amper

PATRICE M. DOMOZYCH

CONTENTS

INTRODUCTION

Lauren shared the following speech at LFG Football Camp in 2014. It is entitled *Feed the Good Wolf.*

"When we started this camp, I was in first grade. On Tuesday, I graduated from high school. Over the last 12 years I have taken a lot of tests. I am sure you have too. It seems like every time you turn around, someone is giving you another test to take.

Besides all the academic tests, I have taken hundreds of medical tests. I know that all of you are also being tested physically and judged on how good of an athlete you are – how fast, how strong, how tall, how much you weigh. You always feel like you have to measure up to some kind of test.

But that is not really true. There are many very important qualities that a test can't measure.

Here are some of them:

creativity

resilience

motivation

persistence

curiosity

humor

endurance

reliability

enthusiasm

empathy

leadership

compassion

courage

sense of wonder

humility

A person who has these qualities will always be successful in life.

I want to read you a short story because it shows how we all have the choice to develop our untestable qualities.

An old Cherokee told his grandson "My son, there is a battle between two wolves inside us all. One is Evil. It is anger, jealousy, greed, resentment, lies and ego. The other is Good. It is joy, peace, love, hope, kindness, empathy and truth."

The boy thought about it and asked, "Grandfather, which wolf wins?" The old man quietly replied, "The one you feed."

Make sure to feed the good wolf."

PATRICE M. DOMOZYCH

FOREWORD

Who is Lauren Loose and why does she have the authority to provide life lessons to anyone at the ripe, old age of 24? This is a valid question. Many of those in their early twenties are likely to be just emerging from college, embarking on careers, or finding solid footing as independent members of society. Lauren is anything but a typical twenty-something.

Lauren Evelyn Loose was born in 1997, the first-born child of John and Marianne Loose, with a genetic disorder called Neurofibromatosis Type I. NF1 is an autosomal dominant genetic disorder which causes tumors to grow along nerves and can affect the development of non-nervous tissues such as bones and skin. It causes tumors to grow anywhere on or in the body and may lead to

11

developmental abnormalities. It is the most common neurological disorder caused by a single gene, affecting one in every 3,000 births. As a result of NF1, Lauren developed brain tumors, bilateral optic and hypothalamic gliomas, just before her second birthday.

Lauren had been on chemotherapy for about four years, with periods of progression and stability, and development of a new lesion in her brain stem, when she developed Evan's Syndrome, a rare blood disorder in which the body makes antibodies that destroy red blood cells, platelets and white blood cells. Chemotherapy for the brain tumors had to be discontinued, and a different chemotherapy coupled with synthetic steroids was introduced to try and control the blood disorder.

In the meantime, during the early years of the new

millennium vision in her "unaffected" eye had deteriorated. She started on a new chemotherapy regimen in the fall of 2004. It kept her stable until January 2006, at which time scans showed that one of her tumors more than doubled in size. She was enrolled in a Phase I clinical trial of Lenalidomide from January 2006 until March 2007, when she developed demyelination (damage to the myelin sheath of the neurons) in her cerebrum and had to discontinue.

In March 2008, at age 11, she was diagnosed with a malignant peripheral nerve sheath tumor, an aggressive soft tissue sarcoma. She had two surgeries to remove the tumor and completed 7 weeks of radiation. In June 2008 after having two strokes, she was diagnosed with severe Moya Moya disease, a progressive narrowing of the blood vessels that feed the brain. She had a double craniotomy with a procedure called pial synangiosis at Children's Hospital of Boston in August 2008 to try and revascularize her brain. She was then diagnosed with Myasthenia Gravis, an autoimmune disease, causing progressive muscle weakness and fatigue. She was in and out of myasthenic crisis and was in treatment with high dose steroids to manage her symptoms.

Like so many children battling brain tumors, both the disease and the side effects of treatment have taken their toll on Lauren. She is blind in one eye and has visual deficits in the other. Her endocrine functions have been affected, requiring treatment, and chemotherapy has damaged some of the nerves in her extremities, causing neuropathic pain. Her permanent teeth developed without roots because of the chemotherapy treatments. Over a two-year span,

Lauren withstood a complicated series of staged dental implant surgeries which gave her a movie star white smile and the ability to enjoy steak and chewing gum again. She has endured more than most do in a lifetime, including surgeries, needle sticks, port flushes, bone marrow biopsies, blood transfusions, chemotherapy infusions, radiation, long hospital stays, physical, occupational and speech therapies, and too many doctor visits to count.

That's just the short list of Lauren's medical history; there are many other unwanted plagues that accompany life threatening illness like fear, insecurity, instability, isolation, loneliness, desperation, insomnia, and depression. But despite all she has been through, Lauren has always remained a happy, enthusiastic, and optimistic person, with an infectious laugh and a true love for life.

After her high school graduation, Lauren began exploring career options at the Orange Ulster BOCES Career and Technical program, especially enjoying cooking classes and proudly earning a Medical Administrative Assistant certificate. She has always taken great joy in helping others and finds treasure in what others may see as ordinary or mundane. No matter the challenges that have been placed before her, she thrives. Her courage, resiliency and relentless spirit are an inspiration to those who know her.

In 2004, Lauren's First and Goal Football Camp and Foundation was established by Lauren's parents to help other families dealing with childhood cancer. The Foundation's mission, to fund pediatric brain tumor research, support pediatric cancer services and families requiring financial assistance, is achieved solely by the work of volunteers. The major annual fundraising event for the Foundation has traditionally been Lauren's First and Goal Football Camp. The camp, a one-day instructional clinic, provides an opportunity for high school athletes to learn, improve skills, showcase talents, experience college coaching and to elevate their future careers as student-athletes at the college level. The camp features instruction by position, individual skill instruction, clinics by guest speakers, a friends and family youth fun tent and keynote speeches.

For years, Lauren has delivered her own speeches to the crowds at LFG's Football Camps beginning in 2004. Initially, these speeches contained just a few words, mostly of thanks, gleefully pronounced into the microphone after a jaunty, hop, skip, and jump from the golf cart which carried an energetic, pigtailed little girl to center field. Through the years Lauren's speeches have evolved. As the camp grew and Lauren matured, so did her thoughts about the work of LFG volunteers, the meaning of the camper's participation, the challenges that we all face and the joys that we all experience as we journey through life. Over time, Lauren's messages developed themes from her unique and profound perspective, which have sparked the idea for this book.

In the next ten chapters, we'll introduce you to Lauren's Life Lessons. We'll also share the quotes of those who have been impacted by her lessons and touched by the ripples of Lauren's Circle of Strength.

Circle of Strength

Anyone who has battled illness knows the importance of a strong support system. In LFG's fight against pediatric brain cancer, we developed Lauren's Circle of Strength. Marianne explains how the String of Strength, a gift from oncology clinic, helped inspire this tremendous network of family, friends - and even strangers- coined Lauren's Circle of Strength.

"Each bead on the string of strength represents an experience during the journey through a child's life with cancer. Some beads symbolize the most unpleasant of experiences such as pokes, surgery, hair loss, chemo and hospital stays. Some beads signify the most beautiful moments, friendships and memories made during the journey. Every bead added to the strand is a tangible and growing testament of the strength, courage and perseverance of the child who earns it.

Lauren started her string of strength about 5 years into her diagnosis. As I sat with her and her nurses and social worker in clinic on the day she started her strand, we tried to piece together the major events that had transpired over the years in order to help her "get credit" for the things that had already happened. As we went through the list, Lauren became more and more excited to collect a giant strand of starter beads.

"'Hair loss, oh yeah, I need that one. Transfusion, yes!! Gimme those!'"

I, on the other hand, became increasingly distressed as I watched the necklace grow. By the time we left clinic that afternoon, Lauren had a smile almost as big as the strand of beads around her neck hanging down to her waist, and I had a giant lump in my throat.

As the weeks went by, and the string of strength grew, it also started to grow on me. I started to see it for what it is - the truth and reality of Lauren's and our family's life with cancer and all the good and bad that goes along with it.

We keep Lauren's string of strength hanging on the giant bulletin board in our kitchen, where we can all see it every day. She wears it with great pride on special occasions, like an exquisite and priceless piece of jewelry. It is her badge of courage, a symbol of her resilience, optimism, and her never quit attitude."

Chapter 1 *Favorite Days*

The hundreds of volunteers who so generously give of their time, efforts, and talents to ensure that LFG Football Camp runs smoothly, do so with insurmountable enthusiasm and energy. Each year, Lauren remarks that the camp is one her most favorite days. For many of us, favorite or memorable days might be marked by special milestone moments like graduations, baptisms, family reunions, weddings, and the like.

Livv Lyfe! Prom

Girls in their senior year of high school spend endless hours perseverating over a date, hairstyles, shoes, jewelry and "the dress" for prom, a  *milestone experience for most. In 2015, Lauren was approaching the end of her high school career and readying for graduation along with her classmates at*

Easton Area High School. For more than a decade, Lauren had been quietly planning for prom with  *longtime friend, Blake Costanzo. The pair had agreed early on that Blake would be Lauren's prom date and as the time drew close, Lauren's family decided to celebrate prom in a most unique way. A Livv Lyfe!! Prom was planned especially for Lauren. Seventeen of the elaborate birthday themes that had been celebrated throughout the years of Lauren's life were incorporated into table centerpieces/themes for the prom party. Special friends, Megan and Jene, styled Lauren and made her a beautiful, custom dream-dress and pulled together the wonderful team of Jenna, Jessica and Therese to complete the look with hair, makeup and a custom bow tie for Blake. It was a beautiful opportunity to be with all the family and friends who have loved and supported Lauren through the most difficult and happiest of times.*

These are days we prepare for after months, maybe even years of diligent organization and anticipation. Our excitement builds as the time for these beautiful life moments draws near and our eagerness for the gathering of our loved ones swells.

Visit with Orlando Bloom

If asked, Lauren would easily mark a favorite day in her life as the day she spent with her hero, Hollywood actor, heartthrob, and absolute sweetheart, Orlando Bloom. It's a captivating story of the magical experience that she and the

Hollywood star spent bonding as friends and trading stories over French toast, bacon and blueberries. Marianne describes the meeting in her CaringBridge (an online communications platform) journal on March 25, 2009 here:

"You people are not going to believe this but.... thanks to the most wonderful, caring and amazingly

persistent friends, and the most trusting and generous new friends on the other end, Lauren lived out her fantasy of meeting her all-time favorite, Orlando Bloom in LA this past weekend. Lauren,

Gracie, Amper and I drove up to Orlando's beautiful house on Sunday for brunch where we were greeted by Sidi, his sweet dog in the driveway. A few seconds later, Orlando was walking down the steps with his arms wide open greeting Lauren and the rest of us with hugs and kisses. He held Lauren's hand and helped her navigate the steps as he took us for a walk up through his beautiful garden, and we all enjoyed a wonderful brunch of Lauren's favorites (including bacon) in his dining room. I think Lauren was partly in shock as she sat next to him, and she forgot most of the things she had planned to ask him, but it didn't matter one bit.

I have to say that I was a bit nervous as to how all of this would work out, and I was afraid that Lauren would be disappointed – I mean really, how could anyone possible live up to  *the expectations that she had built up in her mind? And I have to think that his assistant Adam was sweating bullets, wondering if these potential freaks from the east coast were going to do some irreparable harm to his star client. All I can say is that Orlando Bloom has a new batch of lifelong fans, and hopefully we are of the kind that didn't freak him and Adam out. Not only was he absolutely normal and down to earth, but he was so warm and friendly to all of us and so attentive to Lauren – he even wiped a booger from Lauren's nose! Who does that?!!! Witnessing Lauren's dream come true was one of the greatest gifts I have ever received, and my heart is swelling with gratitude. Thank you, Orlando. Thank you, Adam. Thank you, Kristine and Wendy. Thank you to all of you who hold us up with your prayers, kindness and love."*

Lauren awaits the arrival of camp day each year with the kind of delight and elation that many reserve for life's bigger moments, revealing an important insight. Find something about each day that is exciting. Find something about each day that makes you feel passionate, eager and happy. If you can do this, then you can make each day a favorite day. In one address to campers, Lauren's passion and excitement for the day was echoed in a simple and straightforward manner when she said, "I hope that when you leave today, it will be remembered as one

of your most favorite too."

"Favorite days
are like sunshine
after a storm —
they are warm,
bright,
full of happiness
and hope."

PD, volunteer, age 48

"Live day to day for the right reasons."

Don, coach

"Memories of favorite days give you the fuel to create future favorite days."

Unknown volunteer

"Favorite experiences make my heart full of pride and happiness."

Andrew, Lauren's therapist, age 39

"Today could be the day that you recognize that it quite possibly could be the best day of your life."

Unknown volunteer

"Being positive will get you very far in life."

VF, student, 11

Chapter 2   *Change My Attitude and Mindset*

Lauren's First and Goal Football Camp has attracted more than 30,000 high school student-athletes from over 30 states and 5 countries over a 17-year period since its inception in 2004, making it the largest one-day charitable camp in the nation. Each year, over 400 volunteer coaches representing more than 130 collegiate programs endeavor to deliver an exceptional experience to these eager participants. Through the years some of the most sought-after high school prospects have donned tracking numbers at LFG, honed their skills and hustled to impress college coaches. Athletes come to camp for a variety of reasons and with different goals in mind. Some seek to be challenged as players and others want to learn, grow, and help others.

A Doctor's Note

Being challenged, keeping a positive attitude and knowing resilience is an ongoing practice for Lauren. At age 11, after years of treatments, doctors  *were working on the best way to manage Lauren's endocrine issues. Lauren's mother, Marianne, explained in her CaringBridge journal in 2008.*

"Brain tumors upset the delicate balance of so many of the critical systems and pathways that govern the way the body regulates itself. Lauren's endocrinologist is trying to come up with some way to help Lauren grow, despite the fact that she can't give her growth hormone. All Lauren wants is to be 56 inches tall (4 foot 8 is not asking for much is it?). Those of you who know Lauren know why 56 inches is such a critical number – one has to be at least this height to ride Talon and Great Bear (roller coasters). It is frustrating, but when I read the following note from her doctor this afternoon, I felt a little better. She wrote:

> *"You know, I can prescribe medications to change puberty and growth, and*
> *they don't always work, but I can't change children's attitude and*
> *outlook, and that is the one thing that I admire most about Lauren - her*
> *outlook and positive attitude!! And you too! Lauren is a great girl,*
> *you are very lucky to have her!!! Very true."*

A Beachy Mindset

Journal entry by Marianne Loose — Aug 16, 2008

"*Yesterday was a difficult day for Lauren. They moved us to a step-up room and have been monitoring her closely. At about 7 last night, she started to wake up and have more interest in us. This morning, she is really almost back to her normal personality. She is talking, smiling and she says she feels good. She looks a lot better too. The swelling around her eyes and face is just about gone – she just has a little on the sides of her head where the craniotomies are. The real clue that she is feeling better is that she wanted bacon with her breakfast – Lauren's motto is, "When I'm in the hospital, it's bacon with every meal". Right now, we are pretending we are at the beach – we're watching the TV station that shows a video of the ocean and beach while she eats her bacon.*"

Learning about developing a positive attitude and resilience is one lesson Lauren speaks to when addressing campers. She explains, "Life can be challenging. We all go through times where we feel defeated, make mistakes, are treated unfairly or just have plain bad luck. There may be times when we feel like we are just not good enough. For some of you, maybe you did not get the starting spot on your football team or didn't perform as well as you wanted in front of a recruiter. Maybe you didn't do well on your SAT or your grades are not what you expected them to be this semester. Maybe you got hurt and had to sit out for a season. All of these things can be very discouraging and make you feel angry, upset and just want to give up. For me, my medical problems have made many everyday tasks difficult, painful, and frustrating. I often have to ask for help and get discouraged because I can't be as independent as I want to be. I realize that there are certain things I cannot change, but I can always change my attitude and mindset."

"Walk the path of wanting to change."

Katie, parent of student athlete, 44

"I like challenges,
I like change —
it makes you
grow.
If you embrace
that attitude,
it'll make your
life
so much more
joyful."

Logan, coach

"Be ready
to adapt,
adjust and
keep on
going."

Thomas, volunteer, 75

"Your positive mindset and attitude could be what gets you through your worst days."

RR, coach, 26

"Be open to any and everything that's positive."

Lance, parent of student-athlete, 38

"Attitude

is the

biggest

factor

in

success."

Rob, coach, 31

Chapter 3   *Don't Be Bitter, Make Yourself a Better Person*

Lauren's life, like the lives of many who have endured treatment of a life-threatening illness, can be likened to a roller coaster ride with its unexpected twists and turns, super thrilling highs and gut-wrenching lows.

A Tough Day

Between January and April 2012, at age 15, Lauren was battling numerous health crises including a wicked stomach bug, thyroid issues, myasthenia gravis and crisis, elevated blood pressure, dental consults, and treatments which led to ICU stays and hospitalizations. Although still on shaky ground, her health stabilized, and she was released from the hospital to return home that spring. At that point, she was eager to return to the routines and rhythms of life that are so often taken for granted.

In April, Lauren's mom wrote this in Lauren's CaringBridge journal:

"When I picked Lauren up from school yesterday, she and her teachers said she had a difficult day. She said she couldn't remember the math from last week and the

old English version of Romeo and Juliet made no sense to her at all (you got that right!) By the time we made it out to the car, she was in tears. On the ride home I tried consoling her, reminding her that we all – even those of us without brain tumors and strokes and myasthenia - have days when our brains don't seem to be firing on all cylinders and it is ok. She wasn't having any of it. I think the combination of the steroids and her issues just made for a temporary lapse in her usually positive attitude. This morning, at 5:50 am as I was helping her with her hair, she looked at me in the mirror with a big smile and said, "Today, I am going to MAKE it a good day!" Gooooo Lulu!!!"

This journey through life with cancer has helped Lauren to understand that how you manage comes down to making choices. She says, "You either take what has been dealt to you and allow it to make you a better person, or you allow it to tear you down. The choice does not belong to fate, it belongs to you. You get to choose to look at every setback as an opportunity to make yourself a better person. Don't be bitter, make yourself a better person. And when others see you choosing to be better, they will be inspired to do the same thing."

"Take the struggles in your life and make them the best things in your life."

C, coach, 32

"You have the power in yourself to create the person you want to be no matter the situation."

James, coach, 29

"Positivity

breeds

positivity.

So be positive

and

pass it on!"

Marcus 33 coach

"Improving
is a process.
No matter
how old you get
or
how good you get,
you're
never done."

R, coach

"HAVE SELF-CONFIDENCE SO THAT YOU CAN CHEER YOURSELF ON!"

PETER, STUDENT, 11

"When you turn
setbacks into
opportunities,
you are taking
the good out of bad
and making it
something amazing
or
even life changing!"

EU, student, age 11

Chapter 4   *Show Up*

Showing up provides the opportunity for one to connect with the world. Showing up gives one the chance to build relationships and have experiences that could potentially bring great joy. Showing up may also invoke unease and apprehension for some.

Reach Out

Marianne shares a story of Lauren's gift for showing up in May 2008.

"Today while we were waiting for them to call Lauren in for her treatment, we started talking with one of the ladies we see every day. It turns out her husband is a football coach too, and he and John know each other! He even works with a friend that John worked with at West Point. There is a lesson I have definitely learned from Lauren - unless you stop and make a little effort to step out of your own little world to share a smile or say hello, you miss out on the chance of sharing things that can bring you something wonderful or*

at least brighten your day. She is always reaching out, saying hello, giving a hug, flashing that smile of hers to anyone and everyone – and she has every reason to be walking around with the biggest frown. I realize that not everyone can appreciate it, but I know that her adult 'friends' at radiation do."

Annually, Lauren begins and ends her address to the crowd with gratitude for their presence on a day that means so much to her and to so many others who are battling cancer. She recognizes the effort and bravery that is required to be bold and adventurous. She says, "I've learned that routines can be comfortable, but change can open up great new opportunities in life. It can be scary, but it can also make your life beautiful. I encourage you to always show up. When you force yourself to show up, most of the time you will be glad you did."

"Embrace the fact that you're feeling productive discomfort and that you're doing something to better yourself."

Matt, coach, 55

"75% of the battle is showing up."

Tim, coach, 38

"Showing up is where and when it all starts."

DD, coach

"Every day you
will be faced with
some challenge
or adversity.
If you show up
and
have a great attitude,
you'll see
where life
takes you!"

Allan, coach

"Everyone has the same potential to be courageous and fearless."

Tom, volunteer, 19

Chapter 5   *Discover Your Gifts and Talents*

Since 2004, LFG football camp has fostered the dreams of tens of thousands of high school athletes with hopes of playing football at the highest level. Many LFG alumni have developed their talents, nurtured their gifts, cultivated their skills and gone on to use them to achieve great things in football, college and life.

Honorary Board of Directors

In 2010, US Naval Academy Head Football Coach Ken Niumatalolo connected with the campers in PA with a thoughtful, relevant, and worthwhile message. A standout speaker, and a charismatic, warm, and approachable person, Coach Ken focused on the importance of choices and decisions that young people make, at such a critical time in their lives, that have lasting impacts on their futures. He encouraged campers to align themselves with those who help them to stay true to their goals and appreciate their families and supporters. Most memorably, the former star athlete, coach, husband, father and spiritual leader of the Church of Latter-day Saints, implored campers to live life with an attitude of gratitude. Marianne says, "Coach Ken

expressed a message that focused on the athletes' development as people and embedded the Foundation's mission in his speech. He gets it."

LFG has a distinguished group of coaches on its Honorary Board of Directors, who share their gifts and talents and give their time, generosity, and support to the mission of LFG. They are:

- **Randy Edsall**, *Head Coach,*
  University of Connecticut
- **Luke Fickell,** *Head Coach,*
  University of Cincinnati
- **Kyle Flood,** *Assistant Coach,*
  University of Texas
- **James Franklin,** *Head Coach,*
  Penn State University
- **Archie Griffin,** *President/CEO,*
  The Ohio State University Alumni Association
- **Jim Harbaugh,** *Head Coach,*
  University of Michigan
- **John Harbaugh,** *Head Coach,*
  Baltimore Ravens
- **Darrell Hazell,** *Retired college and NFL coach*
- **Urban Meyer,** *Head Coach,*
  Jacksonville Jaguars
- **Jeff Monken,** *Head Coach,*
  U.S. Military Academy
- **Ken Niumatalolo,** *Head Coach,*
  U.S. Naval Academy
- **Bill O'Brien,** *Assistant Coach,*
  University of Alabama
- **Paul Pasqualoni,** *Special Assistant,*
  University of Florida
- **Frank Solich,** *Head Coach,*
  Ohio University
- **Jim Tressel,** *President,*
  Youngstown State University

Lauren and Randy Edsall   *Kyle Flood and Lauren*

Grace, Ted Daisher, Luke Ronco,
John Harbaugh and Lauren

James Franklin and Lauren

Lauren and Jim Harbaugh

Lauren and Archie Griffin

Paul Pasqualoni

Lauren and Darrell Hazell

Urban Meyer and Lauren

Grace, Jim Tressel and Lauren Luke Fickell and Lauren

Coach Ken and Lauren   *Frank Solich*

Bill O'Brien and Lauren   Coach Monken and Lauren

Lauren recognizes that we each have distinctive and distinguishable gifts that we can use to make the world a better place. She described, "I may not have the gift of physical strength or perfect health, but I have a special gift and desire to spread happiness, love and kindness. I have the gift of being able to work hard and push through challenging situations with a positive attitude. I also have the gift of a loving and supportive family to help me. By sharing my story through this football camp, I can help other children and families living with pediatric cancer."

In her 2014 address to campers, Lauren says, "I believe that we are all born with special and unique gifts and talents. Our job is to discover our gifts and use them in a way to help others, which gives us purpose and life meaning."

"You will, you can do anything."

"Find a way to empower; make them believe they can do anything and hopefully they will empower somebody in the future."

BM, volunteer, 42

"JUST OFFER A RAY OF SUNSHINE."

CINDY, VOLUNTEER, 60

"Show that you can be yourself."

Olivia, volunteer, 11

"When everybody

just

comes together

that just makes you

want to work

toward a good

cause."

Abe, volunteer, 52

"Be

a

blessing."

C., volunteer

Chapter 6   *Be Adaptable*

Adaptation is not only a necessary and required skill of successful athletes that is taught to participants at LFG Football Camp, but it's also an ability that will serve all people well in life. Finding ways to navigate the sometimes-hazardous paths we take as we journey through time requires adjustments in thinking and behavior.

Adapting Expectations

Marianne described a pivotal moment in Lauren's treatment back in 2008. Just when she thought Lauren was set to begin radiation treatment in Boston, Marianne realized that it wasn't going to happen that way. She wrote in Lauren's CaringBridge journal,

"I am very disappointed (that is the 'nice' way of saying it) that she will not be having the Proton radiation in Boston. The team agreed that she was a good candidate, but they were unable to get the CTs, mapping and set up done quickly enough to get her started in time before the benefit of Protons would be outweighed by the risk of waiting so long to start treatment. It is heartbreaking to know that if this was happening 18 months from now, she could be having Protons right across the street from CHOP. Timing is everything, I guess. Anyway - I am trying to accept this huge disappointment and have been trying to think of all of the good things about being in Philly. Lauren already has a

list of ideas, activities and plans for the hours after her treatment, therapies, and appointments. I hope that she will be feeling well enough to do them all."

Lauren has chosen to adapt to the best of her abilities. During her speech to campers in June 2018, Lauren said, "I turned 21 in February. Most people who don't know me assume that I am 10 or 11 years old. The medication and treatment I received for my brain and spinal tumors caused me to stop growing a long time ago. I know that this is the size I am always going to be, and I have chosen to adapt the best I can and make the most of it. For my 21st birthday dinner, I ordered a kids meal and a bottle of beer – you should have seen the waiter's face!" Her story brought the crowd to its feet and Lauren giggled and smiled through her first standing ovation.

"Walk the

path

of wanting

to change

and grow."

Katie, parent of student-athlete, 44

"ADAPT IS HOW YOU CHANGE."

ANDREW, STUDENT-ATHLETE, 16

"In order to advance those goals you have to adjust your means."

Thomas, volunteer, 75

"Change gives

the opportunity

to improve

and to be open to

any and everything

that's positive."

Lance parent of student-athlete 38

"Adapt in life, keep growing, get to your goals."

CG, student-athlete, 17

"*Be coachable,*

teachable

and trainable."

Nick, parent of student-athlete, 35

Chapter 7　　　*Support of a Community*

Many of us have heard the saying "it takes a village to raise a child" and realize the importance of allowing our children a variety of safe and supported experiences that will enable them to grow and develop in a healthy way.

Support from the Circle of Strength

Marianne's CaringBridge journal entry on April 5, 2008 evidences the support of a community.

"Yesterday was such a dreary day, and Lauren and I were feeling it. Today was much better - Lauren got out to watch the Lafayette baseball team beat Bucknell. It was a little chilly, but she enjoyed herself, and being out in the fresh air was just what she needed. I was told by numerous people that if I didn't go work-out this afternoon they were going to kill me, so I reluctantly went to the gym, got the endorphins flowing and felt much better. (I think I am safe for now). Grace wanted to go shopping - just the two of us - it took her about an hour to decide how to spend the 10 dollars that was burning a hole in her pocket, but she came home very content with her selection.

We appreciate all the time spent by so many people

making calls on Lauren's behalf, trying to help the situation in Boston. It just isn't going to happen, and we will have to accept that. Thanks Lynda and Alice for the wise words and reminders regarding acceptance. I'll get there...very soon.

I have Lauren's "hospital school", neurooncology and radiation oncology appointments set up, our name is on the Ronald McDonald house list and we should be able to start up with her PT and OT at the Seashore house next week in Philly.

Gracie's schedule is all worked out thanks to our wonderful neighbors, friends and family. I don't know where to begin to thank everyone for giving so much of themselves to help us. John is in the middle of spring football practice but made some changes to his recruiting schedule so that he can be home at night.

Thanks for all of the messages, good thoughts and prayers for Lauren."

Most athletes who attend LFG Football Camp know what it means to be encouraged, defended, strengthened, and bolstered by a myriad of supporters. Coaches, teachers, family, and friends typically make up the village that nurtures an athlete's success. Lauren sees that having parents, family and friends surrounding her as a gift. At camp, with her Circle of Strength behind her, she encourages us to "Surround yourself with people who love and support you. I don't know what I would do or where I would be without all of the people who support me and love me unconditionally."

"LIVE A ROBUST LIFE BY GIVING AND SUPPORTING OTHERS."

RANDY, COACH, 36

"You can truly get everything you want in life by impacting others and serving others."

James, coach, 47

"None of us have gotten where we are without the people around us."

J, coach

"Knowing that you made someone else's life better because of your efforts
is an unbelievable feeling."

Matt, volunteer, 19

"Strive

to be

a

servant

leader."

R, coach

"You are always better when you put other people before yourself."

Kim, parent of student-athlete, 51

PATRICE M. DOMOZYCH

Chapter 8   *The Bright Side -*
                               Be Thankful

Pausing to look at the bright side of the grimmest situation is a lesson that is hard learned. Lauren understands that in every circumstance there is a bright side.

Radiation and the Presidential Suite

From her CaringBridge journal in 2008 when Lauren first started radiation treatment...

"Lauren had her first treatment and has been throwing up all afternoon. The good news is that she is puking in the bathroom of the Presidential Suite in the mansion side of Ronald McDonald House."

She describes that "A few years ago I was stuck in the hospital for a long time. After a few weeks, it gets hard to know if it's night or day, or even what day it is. I was starting to feel depressed and grouchy, and wanted to go home. One day the dietician came to my room and asked what I had been eating, which was pretty much the same thing every meal, and I was sick and tired of it. She told me that since I had been in the hospital for so long, I could start ordering off the 'special menu' – which included bacon and mozzarella sticks. I started ordering them both with every meal. Now, whenever I have an extended stay in the hospital, I know that there is a bright side and it is golden, fried, and delicious! No matter how bad things may look, there is always something to be thankful for."

"Always expect that good will come."

Sophie, student, 10

"If somebody closes a door, then open a window."

Nancy, volunteer, 71

"Having a positive attitude and outlook can change your outcomes."

Mark, coach, 27

"Even if something seems bad, it can be a gift in disguise."

Kaylee, student, 10

"There is always some silver lining."

Johan, coach, 50

"Being positive is keeping your glass half full."

Chris, coach, 50

Chapter 9   *Dream Big*

LFG Football Camp and Foundation was born of a dream; the dream of the Loose family to make a difference in the lives of children battling cancer. From an early age, Lauren was able to articulate this in the language of a 6-year-old when she wrote, "I have a dream that the kids at Camp Sunshine would have no more brain tumors." This simple, overwhelming, message is what inspired those initial steps to action and the creation of LFG Football Camp and Foundation. In 2017, in her Life Lessons speech, Lauren said, "Don't be afraid to dream big. I always have big ideas and big plans for parties, trips, meals, whatever. Sometimes people think my ideas are ridiculous, but I don't care. I just keep dreaming, planning and doing, and proving people wrong. I also drag other people along with me in my plans, and they always wind up loving it. I am a relentless dreamer."

A Dream Come True

From Lauren's CaringBridge journal written by Marianne 3/26/09…

"A few weeks ago, Lauren and Gracie were invited to the studio of artist Kim Hogan in Bethlehem, PA to work on a glass mosaic piece to be displayed in oncology clinic. Kim is an amazingly talented artist, and she designed the artwork around the idea that children who are patients at clinic would participate in the project by working on the piece with her. The artwork consists of several panels of beautiful glass mosaic that Kim designed to brighten the walls of the Children's Specialty Care Oncology Clinic at Lehigh Valley Hospital. Lauren receives the most wonderful care at LVH as well as Children's Hospital of Philadelphia and she considers the nurses, doctors, and social workers at clinic to be part of her extended family.

The day we were at Kim's studio in early March, each of the four girls participating got to choose a shape and different colored sheets of stained glass. Kim showed the girls how to score, break and cut the glass, then let them go at it. Lauren and Grace each chose butterfly and star shapes to adorn with the beautiful stained glass. When they finished their mini pieces of art, Kim asked the girls to each write a wish on the back of their shape – this way the wishes would be a permanent part of the artwork. Grace wrote "I wish that no one would ever have cancer" and "I wish no kid would get brain tumors". Lauren wrote "I wish no one would ever get tumors" and "I wish I could meet Orlando Bloom" on the back of hers. When she showed me the one about Orlando Bloom, I sort of rolled my eyes at her disapprovingly, but bit my tongue. I had heard that wish pretty much nonstop for the past seven years, and I didn't think it was the most appropriate thing to write on the back of a piece of art, but I also knew it really was a true wish of hers, so I didn't say anything more about it.

I forgot all about it until this afternoon when Nancy, our social worker from clinic, called me. Kim, the artist, and Bruce, her studio mate and photographer, are going to be the featured artists in April at the Banana Factory, which is the building which houses all of the art studios. Their work, including the mosaic piece for the hospital is going to be featured, and Nancy was calling me because they wanted to see if Lauren and Grace could come to the reveal next Friday afternoon to show their stars and butterflies off, wishes and all. Nancy asked what the wishes were, and when Kim told her that one of Lauren's wishes was to meet Orlando Bloom, Nancy couldn't wait to tell them that her wish came true! They couldn't believe it! At the time Lauren made the mosaic and wish in the beginning of March, I had no earthly idea that we would be getting in touch with Orlando's agent to make it happen later the same month.

So, I guess the moral of the story is that we should all wish BIG – if the wish of a 12-year-old girl to meet her real life hero can come true, why can't her other wish of ending cancer come true as well?"

"DREAMS BECOME
YOUR GOALS
AND GOALS
BECOME
YOUR PLANS;
REALLY A DREAM
IS
THE BEGINNING
OF YOUR FUTURE."

CAPRI, VOLUNTEER, 14

"Dreamers accomplish the most."

Chris, coach, 38

"You gotta dream to get anywhere!"

Caleb, student-athlete, 16

"So far,

the only thing

impossible

is impossibility."

Lia, student, 10

"EVERYONE NEEDS TO DREAM."

RICHARD, PARENT OF STUDENT-ATHLETE, 50

"You always need a goal and dreaming is a huge part of goal setting."

J, coach, 32

Chapter 10   *Try New Things*

Vulnerability often presents as a roadblock to many and can provoke even the most skilled and capable people to question their abilities. The possibilities of inadequacy, ineptitude, and failure loom in the minds of most who dare to try new things and push beyond the threshold of typical limits. Lauren feels that the benefit of venturing beyond one's personal comfort zone is worth the initial discomfort that often comes along with it.

In her 2017 "Lauren's Life Lessons" speech she implored campers to "Try new things. Love to learn. Be open to new opportunities to learn, grow and explore. I always like to say "MIGHT AS WELL" when presented with a new opportunity or experience. You never know until you try."

Courage Inside Us All

Lauren was asked to speak about her own courageous spirit in 2010 at a youth empowerment gathering when she was only 13 years old. "People often tell me that I have a lot of courage to face all of the medical challenges I have. I have been fighting  *brain and spinal cancer since I was a baby. But I don't feel like I have any more courage than other people. I just have to use it more than most people. I think courage means being brave and facing your fears. Courage is about not giving up, especially when things get hard. Sometimes courage is about choosing the right thing instead of the easy or popular thing. I know a lot of kids at the hospital with courage. My friend Sterling is totally blind, but he has the courage to continue to do the things he loves like skiing, horseback riding and playing the piano. He doesn't let the fear of what he can't see stop him. When I get scared or nervous there are things I do to boost my courage. I talk about it with my Mom. I pray about it and ask God for help. I surround myself with people who lift my spirits. Everyone carries courage inside them. You just have to make the choice to use it."*

"SHOW UP AND SMILE, EVEN WHEN YOU DON'T ALWAYS HAVE A REASON TO."

ANDY, COACH, 38

"Be brave, ask questions."

Vincent, coach, 42

"Use your courage and you'll feel extraordinary."

Kaitlin, student, 11

"Having the courage to be different can lead to the transformation of a life."

Rich, coach, 32

"Try something new every day."

Robert, parent of student-athlete, 59

"PLAN, GO AND DO WHATEVER; I DO TO BE MY BEST AND SO I GROW."

KEVIN, COACH, 49

ACKNOWLEDGEMENT

On June 2, 2019, a small and enthusiastic team of willing workers, armed with QR codes, Google forms, cell phones and battery chargers, set out on a new, camp day task - to capture the reactions of those in attendance to Lauren's speech themes. Laura and Larry Cudia, from Bohemia, NY, were among these volunteers. Laura joined Lauren's Circle of Strength in 2010, while she served her children's elementary school as the PTA Cultural Arts Program Coordinator, by organizing an author visit for the recently published children's story of LFG Foundation, *Hope Is Here To Stay*. Laura, her husband Larry, and their three children, Courtney, Sean and Nico quickly became the friends who are considered family. The family of five began volunteering at LFG Football Camp PA in 2015, assisting with registration, parking, deliveries, information, data entry, and even the coveted task, believe it or not, of camp clean up and garbage detail. Outgoing, chatty, and friendly, Laura, Larry and Courtney were perfect volunteers to interview attendees for the quotes in this book.

Laura describes her experience as "one of the best days of my life." She explains, "You tell people I do this fundraiser and they say ok I'll do it because everybody wants to do a fundraiser. I tell them, It's really big, it's a big deal… You don't know until you really experience it." Laura, a teacher, was so inspired by her experience volunteering at the camp that she encouraged her students to create a "mind picture" of the 15 young men from Brooklyn, donned in headscarves, muscle hugging, microfiber t-shirts and football gloves, she witnessed gathered together before camp singing Miley Cyrus' "The Climb". Laura said, "And that's exactly it, it's all about the climb."

Larry is astounded by the massive, coordinated effort of volunteers led by a family with plenty of responsibilities assuring the care of their daughter. He says, "I've never seen anybody go to this extent. They've started something that expanded to something pretty impressive and brings notice to their cause." Larry feels that coaches, campers and spectators, with varied backgrounds and experiences, come on camp day with preconceived notions of yet another football camp, but they leave changed for the better, knowing they were part of much more than just another opportunity to soak up the game they love.

LFG foundation is indebted to the following

volunteers for following Lauren's Life Lessons, making LFG a favorite day, showing up, being adaptable, using their gifts and talents, and trying new things:

Hayley Bergin
Laurie Bergin
Mark Bergin
Max Bergin
Courtney Cudia
Larry Cudia
Laura Cudia
Jennifer DiGaetano
Madeleine DiGaetano
Olivia DiGaetano
Kim Hachmann
Rien Hachmann
Tom Mahon
Alene Meehan
Brian Pick

Lauren's First and Goal also recognizes the energy, enthusiasm, and generosity of the members of the Lauren's First and Goal Foundation Board of Directors whose efforts are critical to the success of the Foundation.

Members of Lauren's First and Goal Foundation Board of Directors are:

- **Thomas Atkin**, Principal,
  The Atkin Group, Rear Admiral, United States Coast Guard (Ret.)

- **Dawn Comp**, Senior Athletic Trainer/Rehabilitation Coordinator, Lafayette College

- **Matt Hachmann**, Assistant Football Coach, SUNY Stony Brook

- **John Loose**, Assistant Football Coach, United States Military Academy

- **Marianne Loose**, Director,
  Lauren's First and Goal Foundation, Lauren's mother

- **John Troxell**, Head Football Coach, Franklin and Marshall College

- **Pamela Troxell**, Director,
  Lauren's First and Goal Foundation

PATRICE M. DOMOZYCH

AFTERWORD

The COVID-19 global pandemic caused LFG to make the necessary decision to cancel the 17th annual LFG Football Camp that was to be held in June 2020, in the interest of protecting the health, safety and well-being of attendees, volunteers and the greater community at large. The cancelation was an especially challenging reality for Lauren, who anticipates camp day with similar joy and excitement as that on Christmas morning.

At the time of the writing and publication of this book, the world continues to face the global pandemic. While the current health crisis remains uncertain, LFG Foundation, led by a dedicated, volunteer Board of Directors, remains focused on the mission to fund researchers and support families living with a pediatric cancer diagnosis. This pursuit is only made possible by volunteers and donors who share the Foundation's goals. There are numerous ways one can continue to aid the Foundation during these uncertain times, including purchasing LFG publications, hosting a community fundraising event, or choosing LFG when you shop AmazonSmile (https://smile.amazon.com/gp/charity/homepage.html).

In an effort to provide similar, top notch coaching techniques as given on camp day, beginning in 2021, LFG supporters can subscribe to Coachtube's Lauren's First and Goal store at: https://coachtube.com/laurens-first-and-goal-store.

All proceeds from subscriptions benefit the Foundation.

For more information about Lauren's First and Goal Foundation, please visit our webpage at www.lfgf.org. You may also follow LFG on Facebook www.facebook.com/LaurensFirstandGoal, Twitter www.twitter.com/lfgfootballcamp, and Instagram www.instagram.com/laurensfirstandgoal/.

ABOUT THE AUTHOR

Patrice Domozych is an educator and lives in Oakdale, New York with her husband Rich and three sons, Tom, Mike and James. She and her family have volunteered for Lauren's First and Goal Foundation since its inception in 2004. Patrice is the author of *Hope is Here to Stay* and contributor to and editor of *Manual of Football Drills and Skills*, both LFG publications. She teaches pre-service teachers at St. Joseph's College New York, instructs group exercise, loves to boat, ski, and spend time with her family. Lauren Loose is her niece and goddaughter.

Made in the USA
Middletown, DE
09 July 2021